EMBROIDERY
TIPS & HINTS

EMBROIDERY TIPS & HINTS

Harold Hayes

Guild of Master Craftsman Publications

First published 1996 by
Guild of Master Craftsman Publications Ltd,
166 High Street, Lewes,
East Sussex BN7 1XU

ISBN 0 946819 97 1

Cover photograph by Steve Hawkins
Photography © Jim Pascoe
Illustrations © John Yates

Designed by Ed White

Typeface: Garamond Light

Colour origination by Viscan Graphics P.L.
Printed in Hong Kong by H & Y Printing Co.

Acknowledgements

My thanks to:

Barbara for, amongst other things, Tolerance,

Liz, fairy godmother,

Lindy, editorial midwife,

Jim, photo magician,

and Kathlyn, who staves off midnight.

Contents

Introduction

During the years I have spent embroidering, I have developed a number of devices and expedients which help to minimize the frustrations which can occur, and which put off people who would otherwise get as much enjoyment from the craft as I do.

Logically, one would set these devices out in sequence, from the selection of the design to the presentation of the completed work, but logic does not necessarily apply to embroidery, and I have arranged them alphabetically.

I hope that these tips will help others to have fun, as I do, with needle and thread.

Adapting Equipment

Squidge is my word for soft foam packaging, or polyurethane foam. I still have bits I hoarded when unpacking some computer discs 20-odd years ago, and new supplies occasionally arrive, as protection for delicate, packaged things. If you have no foam packaging or polyurethane, pieces of soft plastic sponge can be substituted.

Squidge – polyurethane foam used to stop equipment rattling or slipping

I put squidge to many uses. Things which slide about when I want them to stay still (pincushions, bead trays, etc.) have slips of squidge stuck to their bases to stop their bad habits; things which rattle when they shouldn't, (working frames, etc.) have bits of squidge stuck to their undersides, not only to avoid the rattle, but also to stop them skidding; and clamps, such as those used for special lamps and other equipment, can have bits of squidge fixed to them to avoid damage to furniture. Embroidery apart, equipment such as typewriters and word processors benefit from having squidged feet.

Adhesives

There are many adhesives available, and all have their specific uses, but I find myself using only a very limited number.

Lastex emulsions such as Copydex, I find tend to penetrate fabrics too easily, and to remain tacky even after drying. Rubber solutions, such as Cow gum, have occasional uses, but also penetrate fabrics too well. Balsa cement and other quick-setting glues are really only useful for special effects.

I use Evostik Impact Adhesive for a specific purpose. I usually buy it as Evostik Wood Adhesive, in 500ml (1pt.) bottles, but it is available in small dispensers from most haberdashers, as Hi-tack or other proprietary names. Undiluted, as a sticky cream, I use it to seal the edges of embroideries which are to be cut out as appliqué motifs. With a fingertip, I smear it into the edges from the back. This seals the ground fabric so that it doesn't fray, and also fixes the embroidered threads so that if, in cutting out, the odd thread gets snipped, the remainder will stay put.

For most purposes I stick to PVA emulsions, available in several forms and under many names. I use PVA emulsion, diluted with two parts of water (or thereabouts - the strength is not critical) to stiffen

A choice of adhesives

lightweight fabrics and prevent them from fraying, particularly for appliqué work, where I want to avoid turning the edge in. The fabric remains flexible and easy to sew on.

Incidentally, I never rely on adhesives for permanent fixing of textiles, such as collage, but always stitch for final results.

See also
Mounting Motifs
(page 30)
Sealing Edges
(page 39)

Adhesive Tapes

I seldom use the transparent Sellotape, except to join sheets of paper for a large pattern.

Masking tape I use quite often. I use it to locate a piece of cloth within a working frame, in preparation for lashing. For large works, I stick a short piece of masking tape at each corner of the frame, and at intervals along the sides, removing the tape and returning it to the reel for re-use as the stitching reaches each piece.

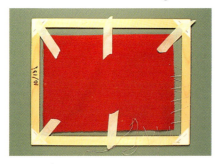

Fabric taped in position for lashing

Double-sided tape is very useful. For patchwork I use little pieces to locate patterns to fabric, in preparation for tacking. I also use it: to locate a finished work to its mounting board or frame, enabling relocation if necessary (it unsticks without leaving a residue); for covering buttons, keeping the fabric attached to the button while I stitch it on; and for holding the pivot point to the machine bed when I am using circular stitching. I have even used double-sided tape instead of lashing, for embroidering parasol panels on a triangular working frame.

Double-sided tape locating patches to patterns

Of all the uses to which I put tapes, however, none is permanent. All tapes deteriorate with time, become brittle and lose their adhesion, so I make sure I remove them whenever possible, and use stitches for the permanent fixing.

See also
Circular Stitching
(page 10)

Working with larger embroideries may involve the risk of your top hand resting on the work and causing unwanted stretching of the fabric. I avoid this by using a bridge – a piece of wood, about 2in (50mm) wide, which I can lay across the corner of the working frame. This bridge supports my hand, or at least reminds me not to rest it on the embroidery.

Using an armrest to protect fabric

Backing Cloth

A finished embroidery panel or picture, duly lashed to a frame, card, or board, still looks untidy from the back. I always cover the lashing with a backing cloth for appearance' sake, and as a supplement to the lashing to secure it.

Oddments of curtain lining are ideal for backing, but almost any fabric will do. I cut a piece a little larger than the work, turn in and iron the edges for an exact fit, pin the corners of the backing in place, add further pins at intervals around the edge to hold it steady, then overstitch through the backing and the edge of the work, all the way around.

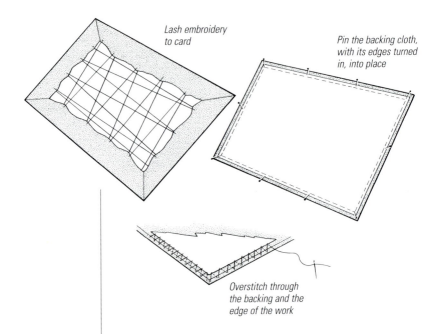

Lash embroidery to card

Pin the backing cloth, with its edges turned in, into place

Overstitch through the backing and the edge of the work

Bead Storage

I find it irritating when equipment and materials will not stay where I put them, so I have developed a special container for storing beads. It is a shallow plastic lid into which I have glued a piece of short-pile cotton velvet, shown in A. I can decant beads, sequins and other 'mobile' things into this, they will stay put, and I can pick them out easily with the tip of a needle as I want them. To stop the container flipping, I weight the lid by fixing a piece of something heavy to it, and I glue plastic foam or pile fabric on its base to stop it skidding, as seen in B.

A *Bead tray in use*

B *Squidge backing*

See also
**Adapting
Equipment**
(page 2)

S cissors are such an important tool, it is well worth keeping them in first class condition. The first requisite is to keep each pair for its own specific purpose – never use fabric scissors for cutting paper, as the filler used in paper acts as a mild abrasive and will eventually grind away the cutting edge of your scissors.

My personal collection of scissors includes: 10in (25.5cm) cutting-out; 8in (20cm) pinking; 5in (13cm) general purpose; 3½in (9cm) fine-pointed embroidery; and 4in (10cm) curved (nail), for cutting funny shapes. At my workbench I keep 12in (30.5cm) shears (wallpaper); 10in (25.5cm) shears; 9in (23cm) general purpose; and 4in (10cm) embroidery. At my sewing machine, I always keep a pair of spring-open snips for cutting off.

Avoid straining scissors. If they don't cut easily, use a stronger or heavier pair, as straining can damage the pivot or distort the shape of the blades. Although some modern scissors have flat blades, the traditional tool has each blade slightly curved, to give a single, clear contact point (the shear point), which travels along the blades as they close. If the blades are distorted in any way, the shearing is affected.

A Pivot screw

To avoid damage to your scissors, keep them clear of pins, staples, and other hard or abrasive materials.

If scissors lose their keenness, do something about it rather than suffer the frustration of using an inefficient tool. Often, the only fault is that the pivot has worn loose. If the pivot is a screw, as shown in A above, it can be

B Rivet

tightened by turning it bit by bit. Keep the blades open, and test frequently, turning until the blades move firmly together, without being stiff. Once the correct setting has been found, it can be fixed by using a centre punch between the edge of the screw and the blade. Position the point of the punch at the edge of the pivot, and give it a sharp blow with a hammer, making a dimple which will stop the pivot moving out of position.

With small scissors, what appears to be a screw pivot is usually a rivet, as seen in B (above). These can be tightened by tapping them against any solid metal object, keeping the blades open, and checking stage by stage until the closure is firm but not tight.

If re-setting or sharpening is required, find a competent cutler, not an itinerant knife grinder. I do my own, but it does require a certain amount of knowledge, the right equipment, and a lot of care.

Circular Stitching

Sometimes circular stitching is necessary. I use it to finish off circular coasters, placemats or tablemats. Using it very seldom, I never remember where I have put the required gadget, so I improvise.

A Pivot pin located

I measure the diameter of the circle I want, halve it to find the radius, and mark that distance from the needle, to the side and directly in line with it, on the bed of the machine. I then take a flat-headed drawing pin, stick a patch of double-sided tape to it, and stick the drawing pin, point up, to the mark on the machine bed. I find the centre of my embroidery and push this onto the drawing pin, then add a circle of card, pushing it onto the drawing pin as well, to help keep the embroidery in place. I then cover the point of the drawing pin with a small piece of cork. All that is needed then is to stitch around the item, usually with a zig-zag stitch to simulate overlocking. The machine turns the embroidery around, while I hold it flat under the card. A, above, shows the drawing pin fixed in position, and B, below, shows the embroidery and card assembled, and stitching underway.

When I have finished the sewing, I trim off the excess and, if necessary, singe the cut edge to neaten it.

B Circular stitching and trimming

See also
Adhesive Tapes
(page 4)
**Singeing to
Remove Fuzz**
(page 41)

Colour Fastness Test

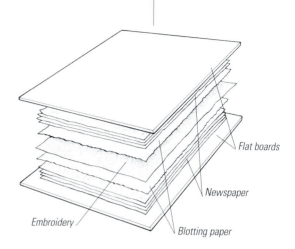

Before cleaning an embroidery, it is necessary to establish whether the work is colourfast. Wet two sheets of clean white blotting paper with water, and sandwich the article between them. Sandwich this between several layers of newspaper, and sandwich the whole between flat boards, such as cutting boards or trays. Place a heavy weight on top to ensure good contact, and leave to dry for about 24 hours.

Flat boards

Newspaper

Embroidery

Blotting paper

Checking for colour fastness

If the colours are not fast, they will stain the blotting paper as the moisture migrates and carries the particles of dye with it. If no significant colour appears, follow the same procedure, using a mild solution of soap to wet the blotting paper. If this is satisfactory, wash the article in that solution by the method described under Washing & Dusting Embroideries.

If the colour is not fast in a soap solution (which is alkaline), try again in a solution of mild synthetic detergent such as washing-up liquid, adding a teaspoonful of acetic acid (white vinegar) to acidify it. Some dyes are fugitive in alkalies, but fast in acids.

If all aqueous solutions fail, the article will have to be dry-cleaned, i.e. washed in a volatile spirit instead of water. The most readily available of these is white spirit. This is effective, but the residue takes a while to evaporate and even longer to lose its smell. Wash the article in white spirit, mop up as much of the excess as possible, and leave to dry, preferably out-of-doors, until the smell has gone.

See also
Washing & Dusting Embroideries
(page 63)

Combining Yarns

Sometimes, particularly when creating heavily textured surfaces, I want a yarn thicker than any I have available, or I want to combine a number of yarns. In such cases, I use my special gadget, composed of a saucer, two loops of string, sticky tape and a safety pin.

I fix the two loops of string to the saucer with sticky tape, and use the safety pin to hold them where they cross, as shown in the diagram. I cut equal lengths of the yarns I wish to combine, knot them together, and slip the knot onto the safety pin. Then, holding the saucer above the floor, I spin it until I have the desired amount of twist in the yarns. For short lengths I can hold the whole set-up with the ends at head height; for longer lengths I tie the free ends to a distant door knob, and get the twist to travel along the yarns by alternating my supporting hand.

The doubled yarns can be wound onto a card and used directly, but in that case, must be held firmly to avoid untwisting. Usually, I dampen the doubled yarns and leave them to dry under light tension, to set in the new twist.

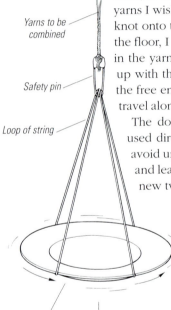

Yarns to be combined

Safety pin

Loop of string

Saucer

Cops & Spools

Cops of about 5,000 or 10,000 yards or metres of thread, and spools of about 500 or 1,000 yards or metres are a very economical way of buying threads that you use a lot. However, they both have the disadvantage of tending to fall and roll away. To stop this happening, I cut circular cards a little larger than the diameter of the cops, and glue one to the base of each cop. For spools I do the same, but fix the spool to the card with a patch of double-sided tape so that the spool can be removed for storage (and the disc re-used). I usually use card cut from a breakfast cereal box, but I sometimes use pieces cut from an ice cream carton – it depends what I have available. Such cards can be used to stabilize any unstable thing.

Spray, cop and spool on stabilizing discs

Creating Texture

Some of my work involves making heavily textured surfaces, and I use a number of materials and techniques to do this.

Strips of cloth (jersey cut in any way, woven cloth cut on the bias or cut straight, with the edges frayed to leave a fringe) can be sewn down with a single line of stitches, bringing the strips close together so that the edges stand up. The sample in A, below, shows pink-cut squares, jersey strips, and cloth with the edges frayed.

Small pieces of cloth (round or square or any shape, straight-cut, fringed or pink-cut) will give depth and texture when sewn down close together with a single, central stitch. You can even sew one piece onto another. In all cases, the pieces should be sewn closer together than their size, so that their edges stand up. Greater depth can be achieved if the pieces are sewn onto a spongy ground – apply a layer or two of old knitwear or similar fabric before stitching them down.

For special textured effects, fabrics can be manipulated

A *Creating texture using different materials and cutting techniques*

before being applied to the ground cloth. They can be pleated, ruched, bunched, stretched, torn or cut.

Finally, don't forget the role the threads themselves can play in creating texture. I used many different materials for the cherry blossom shown in B, below. Use fine threads, coarse threads, gauze, cords, braid, ribbons, and multiple yarns, and experiment with different ways of stitching. The possibilities are endless!

B Threads of many different materials can be used to create texture

See also
Combining Yarns
(page 12)

15

Damping Materials

I sometimes use a sponge for damping, and for multiple yarns, double or plaited, I use a scrap of very wet terry towelling, lightly applied. I fix one end of the yarn to a stable surface with Blu-Tack, hold the yarn out straight, and run the damp terry towelling along it.

For most damping however, I use a pistol-grip mist spray (the sort used for spraying pot plants), with the nozzle adjusted to give a fine mist, without droplets. I find this much more reliable and controllable than using the steam facility on my iron, which requires frequent re-filling and is liable to spit unwanted drops of wetness or deposits. With the mist spray I can apply as much or as little water as I want.

The one problem with my pistolgrip spray is its tendency to fall over. To overcome this, I have stuck a circle of plastic to its base. I always use plastic (from the lid of an ice cream container) rather than the card I sometimes use for cops, as it is easy to spill water when re-filling the mister.

Damp
terry towelling

Blu-Tack

Multiple yarn

See also
Cops & Spools
(page 13)

Defining a Straight Line

O ne use I have for Lastex, or shirring elastic, is to define a straight line, for example, locating the edge of a finished work before removing it from the working frame. I put a pin at each corner of the work, stretch a Lastex thread between the pins, and tack across the work alongside the Lastex. This defines the edge on the front and back.

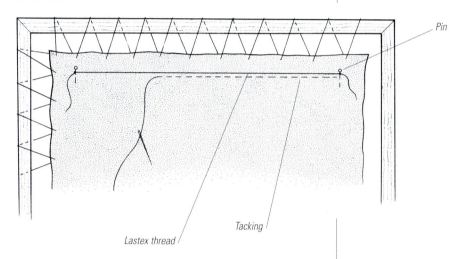

Pin

Tacking

Lastex thread

See also
Double Ground
(page 18)
**Temporary
Tensioners**
(page 51)

Double Ground

Sometimes one would like to use a special fabric as a ground for embroidery, which is in itself unsuitable – too weak to support the stitching, or too stretchy to avoid cockling, or otherwise inappropriate. It can still be used, however, if doubled with a strong fabric, leaving the decorative material to be seen, with the firm fabric below to support the embroidery.

Stretch a piece of strong fabric onto a working frame. Work it a bit to take up the initial stretch, and re-tension it as described under Tensioning Finished Work. Place the desired, but weaker cloth over this, and fix it in position with Lastex tensioners or tacking. This will keep it in position with the minimum of stress while you work the embroidery, stitching through the double fabric.

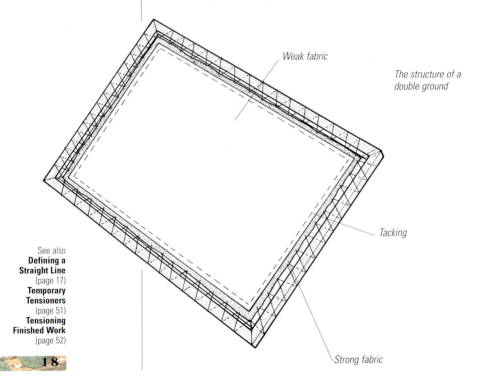

Weak fabric

The structure of a double ground

Tacking

Strong fabric

See also
**Defining a
Straight Line**
(page 17)
**Temporary
Tensioners**
(page 51)
**Tensioning
Finished Work**
(page 52)

Drawing Out a Single Thread

S ometimes I want a single strand from a two-ply or
three-ply yarn. Singling out one strand from the six of
a stranded cotton is simple, but taking one from a multiple
yarn can be tricky, as the tail tends to twist into a knot.
I have seen people holding the end in their teeth,
between their knees, and in many other weird places.

My answer is a bulldog clip. I attach one to the end of
the yarn, and allow it to spin to take the twist, while I peel
off the single desired strand. I unclip it to remove the
strand completely, and then attach it to the scrumpled
strands, and allow the yarn to spin again, to restore the
natural twist.

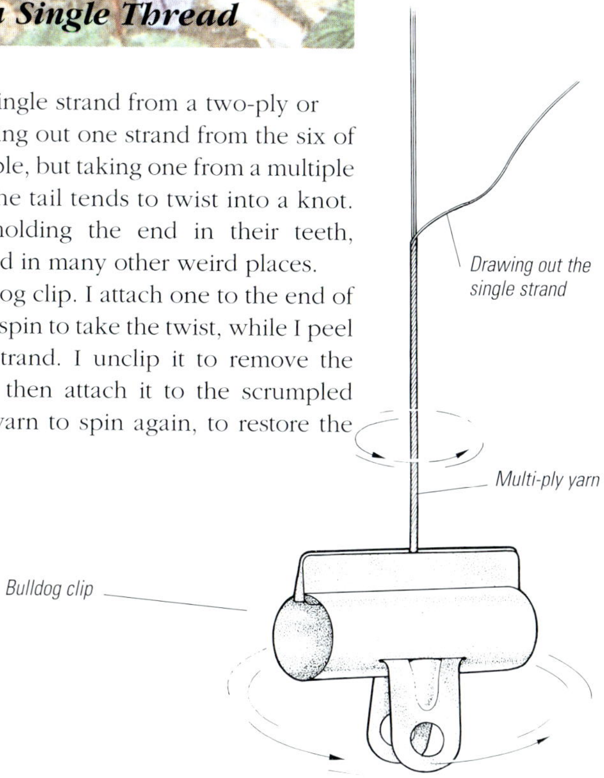

Drawing out the single strand

Multi-ply yarn

Bulldog clip

See also
Temporary Tacking
(page 50)

Evening Tension

A stable ground fabric (one which does not distort under tension) can be lashed into a working frame without undue problems, but a stretchy fabric will show alternative areas of tight and loose tension where the lashing occurs. To overcome this, prepare the ground fabric by machining onto each edge, a strip of bias-cut fabric about 1½-2in (38-51mm) wide, and take the lashing stitches into that. Remember to allow for the extra size when selecting or making the working frame.

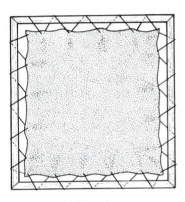

Stable ground fabric, lashed
directly into frame

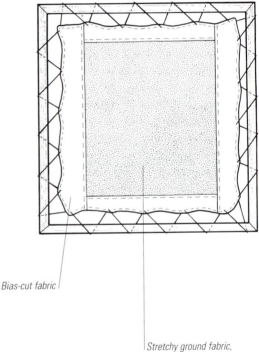

Bias-cut fabric

Stretchy ground fabric,
lashed into frame through
bias-cut edging

See also
Frames
(page 21)

Frames

For almost every sort of embroidery I do, I like to work on a ground of stretched fabric: I can see what I'm doing, I can support the work so that I can use both hands to embroider, instead of using one as a clamp, and the tension of a taut ground fabric evens out any tendency I have to vary the tensions of the stitching.

I cannot get on with hoops. However carefully I set the work in a frame, and however tightly I screw it, the fabric always slackens with use and has to be re-fixed. Instead, I use frames into which I lash the working fabric.

Frames are easy to make. No elaborate joints are needed, as the tensions of the workpiece hold the frame together. For a square or rectangular frame, cut four pieces of thin hardwood, about 1 x $\frac{1}{8}$in (25.5 x 3mm), to lengths at least 1in (25.5mm) longer than the sides of the fabric to be worked on. Cut across each end at an angle of 45°, to form a mitre. An easy way to do this is to mark a square at the end, mark its diagonal, and cut across this. I suggest hardwood because it is readily available from DIY stores, but any wood will do. If you use softwood, it is a good idea to use pieces that are a little thicker.

Assembling the frame isn't difficult. Lay the pieces out together and, across each corner, front and back, glue a piece of thin firm card or strong paper. If you happen to have a friend in the printing trade, ask them for scrap photolitho plates and use them instead. They are thin aluminium alloy sheets which can be cut with strong scissors or scored with a craft knife and snapped.

Frames of other shapes can be made in the same way, using the appropriate angles at the corners. For baubles I

Cut line

Card

Cut across diagonal

Continued...

use a five-sided frame, for hexagonal patches, six-sided, and to approximate a circle, eight to twelve sides. For parasols I use a triangular frame.

For rigidity, the larger the frame, the thicker the timber required. Above about 18in (45.5cm), it is advisable to use thicker timber, and for a frame over 3ft (91cm) long, the timber must be thick enough not to warp under tension. For such large frames, the corners should be reinforced with panel pins.

These frames can be used again and again. I have accumulated quite a stock of different sizes from which I can select one for almost any new project.

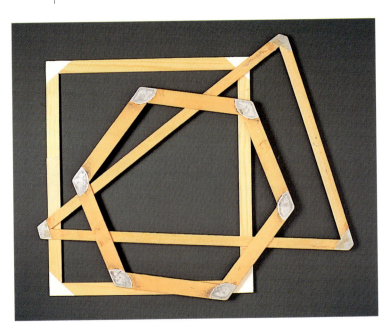

Typical working frames

Fred: Catching Scraps of Thread

My constant workmate is Fred. Early on I found that odd bits of thread (unpickings, trimmings, frayed ends, etc.) tended to gravitate to the carpet, and that once there they were difficult to see, and even more difficult to pick up. Even the vacuum cleaner tended to scrub them into the pile rather than suck them out. The logical answer was to bring a piece of carpet to the threads, hence Fred.

He is, to the uninformed, a piece of carpet 3-4in (7.5-10cm) across. To stop him skidding, he has a thin layer of plastic foam on his back. He lives on the piece I am working on, or alongside it, and he takes all the bits of thread which would otherwise fall to the ground. He is particularly good at removing those bits which stick to the rough skin of my fingers. Periodically, I rub a damp finger across him to collect the threads, and transfer them to the wastepaper basket.

Fred in use – and his foam underside

See also
**Adapting
Equipment**
(page 2)

23

Hinge for Two-Way Folding

I t is often useful for screens and other equipment to have a hinge that can fold fully in each direction. This is how I make such a hinge.

1 Take the two panels to be so hinged, lay them end-to-end, and round off their adjacent edges.

2 Fix short strips of webbing, strong tape, cloth, or leather across the join. Glue or staple each strip to one panel only, alternating from left to right as you go.

3 Turn the panels over, and bring the loose ends of the strips through to the top. Fix the loose end of each strip to the panel it is resting on. Again, this should alternate from left to right.

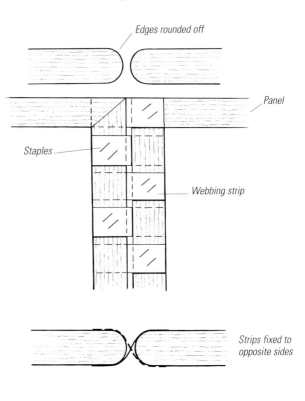

Edges rounded off

Panel

Staples

Webbing strip

Strips fixed to opposite sides

Jumbo Clips

I noticed that the open air market traders used very strong spring clips to hold the tarpaulins tight over their stalls. On one (and only one) occasion, there were some for sale at an 'everything for 50p or £1' stall, and I bought four. Having given a pair to a friend, and wanting more, I later asked where they were available, and a helpful stallholder gave me some.

I use jumbo clips for any temporary, heavy-duty fastening, for example: holding things together while glue sets; holding a section of bedspread in a frame while quilting it, rather than setting up a full quilting frame; holding down 'praying mantises' when supporting a working frame; and fixing the working frame to the mantises.

Such heavy-duty equipment is not usually associated with the craft of embroidery, but it is worth keeping an open mind and borrowing from other crafts and occupations, if they can help with needle and thread.

Patchwork clipped to frame for quilting

See also
Supporting the Workpiece
(page 48)

Knotted Threads

After threading a needle, I draw the thread between a fingertip and a fingernail to straighten any kinks and to confirm by touch that there are no knots or faults. Even so, there is often a tendency for the tail end of the thread to whip itself into a knot as you work, particularly with a single thread of stranded cotton or spun synthetic yarn. The sequence is that the tail whips into a pig's tail, then starts to fray, the frayed end clings to the main thread, and finally into a knot.

This can be avoided if, after threading the needle, the free end is drawn across a piece of beeswax, and the last ¼ in (6mm) is cut off to leave a clean end.

Beeswax is also invaluable for stiffening the end of a difficult yarn to facilitate threading the needle. Again, cut off the last ¼ in (6mm) to leave a clean end.

The tail starts with a pig's tail

After a while the end frays…

and attaches itself to the main thread…

eventually knotting around it

Avoid this by waxing the tail

Lashing

With most stable fabrics, a lashing stitch every 1in (25mm) or so is sufficient to hold the ground fabric securely in the working frame. However, with a stretchy fabric, it may be necessary to add bias strip to each edge before lashing it into the frame to ensure the tension is even.

Locate the fabric within the frame and fix it temporarily with bits of masking tape. Lash the fabric to the frame to fix it permanently, and remove the tape as the stitching progresses.

I use polyester button thread for lashing. If you use a crewel needle, it is not necessary to finish off each thread: you can start a new thread by tying it to the end of the old length, as a reef or granny knot will pull through the hole made by a crewel needle quite easily. The lengths of thread can eventually be unpicked for re-use.

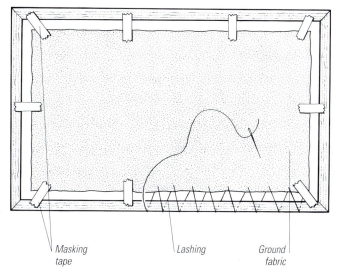

Masking tape   Lashing   Ground fabric

Having completed the lashing, go around again, pulling taut any slack so that the fabric is drum tight. After some initial working on the fabric, slack may develop and it may be necessary to do this again, chasing the slack around from start to finish, but thereafter the tension should be retained. Fasten off the lashing thread by sticking it to the frame with a piece of masking tape.

See also
Adhesive Tapes
(page 4)
Evening Tension
(page 20)

Lighting

Always ensure that you work in good lighting, and that it is good general lighting rather than intense local lighting. Too great a contrast between the light on your work and the general lighting is a strain on your eyes, making your irises open and close each time you look up from, and back to your work. Too intense a light is also tiring on the eyes. If, when you close your eyes you can still see an image, the light has been too strong. The retained image indicates that the receiving cells are tired and trying to recover. If you use a spotlight, table lamp, angle-poise or other local lighting, use a low-watt bulb and keep the general level of lighting high.

A strong light from one direction casts heavy shadows, so avoid working in direct sunlight. Sometimes it helps if you can site a mirror, or a sheet of white paper, to catch some of the directional light and reflect it in the direction you want. A simple mirror of kitchen foil stuck to cardboard, with a foot folded back so that it can stand on the table or on the workpiece itself (as shown), is easily made and quite effective. Even wearing a bib of white cloth can help to reflect light.

Card and foil mirror in use

Whatever the lighting, avoid working too long without a break of at least a few seconds, looking out of the window or across the room, in order to change the focus and give the eyes a rest.

Mitred Corners

I am told that I don't mitre fabric corners as other people do when mounting an embroidery or preparing a backing cloth. The conventional way is to fold the edges in, and then to pull the corner out and re-position it as flat as possible. I fold the corner in first and then the sides, and the mitre is made, quite flat.

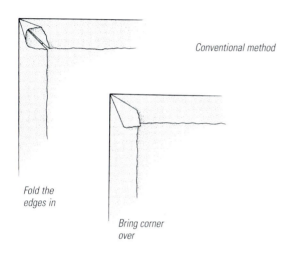

Conventional method

Fold the edges in

Bring corner over

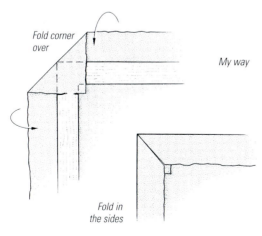

Fold corner over

My way

Fold in the sides

Sometimes I embroider motifs for use as appliqué decorations on garments, or for mounting on hair combs, brooches or pins. When I use motifs for appliqué, I normally seal the edges before cutting the motif and ground fabric.

For mounting motifs on a brooch or other separate item, I use Evostik Impact Adhesive to first back the motif with aluminium sheet, and then to mount the backed motif on the brooch or other item. With my fingers protected by a glove, I smear the adhesive all over the back of the motif, and over a piece of thin aluminium sheet, or photolitho plate when I can get one (shown in A). I have a friend in the printing trade who sometimes supplies me with used plates. Aluminium sheets come in various sizes: the larger sheets are of medium weight aluminium, while the smallest sheets, about 12 x 15in (30.5 x 38cm), are very thin aluminium which can be cut with an ordinary pair of scissors.

Having stuck the embroidery firmly to the metal (B), the motif can be cut out quite readily (C), leaving it semi-rigid, and suitable for mounting on a brooch, pin, comb or any item you choose (see butterfly pin below). If, after cutting the motif out, there is any fuzz of unwanted fibres, these can best be removed by singeing.

Butterfly mounted on pin

A Smear the glue on the back of the embroidery and the aluminium sheet

B Stick the metal to the embroidery

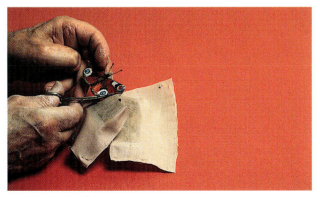

C Cut the motif out

See also
Sealing Edges
(page 39)
**Singeing to
Remove Fuzz**
(page 41)

Mounting Panels

I have two distinct ways of mounting an embroidery as a panel: without stress, and stretched.

For a delicate embroidery, particularly an old one, I mount the piece without placing any stress on it, by stretching a piece of strong fabric, larger than the embroidery to be mounted, tacking the embroidery to it with as many invisible tacking stitches as are needed to hold the embroidery in place, and then mounting the whole thing as a stretched embroidery. In this way, the stretch is taken up by the strong fabric, and places no strain on the embroidery.

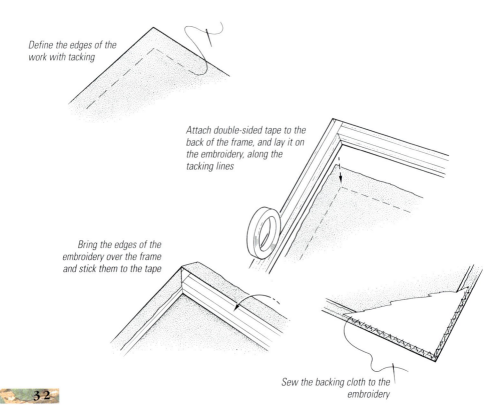

Define the edges of the work with tacking

Attach double-sided tape to the back of the frame, and lay it on the embroidery, along the tacking lines

Bring the edges of the embroidery over the frame and stick them to the tape

Sew the backing cloth to the embroidery

For an embroidery which is strong enough to be kept under tension, and which may cockle once it has been removed from its working frame, I use a different method. I mount it on a firm piece of hardboard, or a simple frame made to measure, and stretch it by stitching through the embroidery and onto a backing cloth.

I start by defining the edges of the finished work before taking it off the working frame. For this I enlist the help of Lastex yarn, and tack in straight lines all around the work. After this, I attach narrow strips of double-sided tape to the back of the board or frame, lay it on the back of the embroidery, guided by the tacking lines, bring the edges over and stick them to the tape. I then turn the work over, adjust the positioning if necessary, and ensure that everything is firmly stuck down. Finally, I cut a piece of backing cloth, fold in and iron the edges, and sew this to the embroidery, stretching it as necessary to prevent the fabric cockling.

For delicate embroidery doubled with a strong ground fabric, this backing and stretching is done in the same way.

See also
Defining a Straight Line
(page 17)
Double Ground
(page 18)
Temporary Tensioners
(page 51)

Pile Combs

The traditional way to make nice even pile in embroidery, is to stitch over a knitting needle, eventually withdrawing it and either leaving the loops uncut, or cutting them to give a tufted texture. This works well, but is tedious, so I developed the Pile Comb, which is, in effect, a number of knitting needles side-by-side.

Cocktail sticks, pieces of barbecue skewers, matches or any such material can be used. I space 10 or 12 sticks, about 2½-3in (63-76mm) long, with short ½in (12mm) pieces, glue them together and neaten the finished comb with some fancy sticky tape work.

A *Varying thicknesses of cut pile*

Using straight, plain stitches over a comb will build up an area of pile quite quickly. Stitches may be regularly spaced, or spread randomly, and may be done using a single thread, or multiple threads, stitching over one or a number of combs, combining different colours and even different materials.

The pile may be cut with a sharp knife, pressing the knife down onto the wood of the comb, cut with fine scissors after removing the comb, or left uncut. Sample A, shows cut pile that has been stitched over a single comb, a double comb, and a triple comb. Sample B shows both cut and uncut pile.

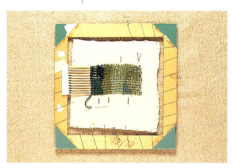

B *Pile may be cut or left uncut*

Pincushion

ailors, couturiers, and others who need pins while on the move, fix a pincushion to their clothing. Embroiderers usually have a pincushion to hand, but it has to be picked up and held to remove or replace a pin. I found this irritating, so I made a cushion heavy enough to stay in a fixed place, so that I could use it with only one hand. I now have several of these.

To make such a pincushion I first find a tin lid, about 3in (76mm) in diameter. I then glue layers of expanded polystyrene sheeting together until I have a block thick enough for me to carve from it, a hemispherical dome to fit the tin lid. I carve it out with a sharp knife, and finish it with coarse sandpaper. I fill the lid with dry sand to weight it, stick the poly-styrene dome to the lid, and cover the whole with Jersey cloth. To the bottom of the lid I stick a thin layer of squidge to stop it slipping.

Layers of polystyrene, carved to form a dome

Tin lid, filled with dry sand

Thin polystyrene strip

With the weighting and the squidge to hold it in place, I can remove or replace a pin with one hand: the pincushion will stay put, whether it be on the work table, the actual piece, or any other surface.

See also
Adapting Equipment
(page 2)
Supporting the Workpiece
(page 48)

Plastic Slip

Working on a tightly stretched ground brings its own problem: if one needs to make a running stitch, or to stitch in the end of a thread, the tension of the ground tends to make the point of the needle dig in and not come clear to be pulled out. I keep a slip of plastic handy, which I place under the needle tip to prevent it going in again while I pull it through.

In order to make the slip clearly visible, I have stuck a strip of reflective paper across it. This is useful for any items that can be hard to find.

The needle is kept visible and accessible with a plastic slip

Posture

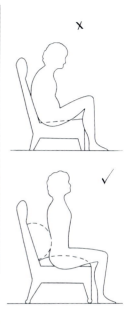

If, when you pause in embroidering, you feel the need to tilt your head and press your shoulders back, your posture has been wrong. It is significant that the Principal of the Royal School of Needlework has said that the first thing she teaches her students is the need for correct posture.

Ideally, one's posture when working should be, in all respects other than the legs, the same as when walking, i.e. a straight spine requiring the minimum of muscle exertion to keep it in position.

Consider first the chair. This should support you with your thighs almost horizontal, but with the seat not so far forward as to restrict blood flow behind the knees. What is required is a firm, but comfortable seat, at a height appropriate to the length of your lower leg, and not too deep from back to front. If your back is unsupported, you will need a firm lumbar cushion to fill the gap and remind you, every time you sit back, to keep an erect position.

Consider then the position of your work. It should be at a height and distance from you consistent with maintaining your posture, while being at a distance from your eyes to facilitate ease of focusing, and within proper handling distance.

I spend many hours a day embroidering and I cannot remember when I last had aching muscles. I have modified my chair with additional seat and lumbar cushions, and I use a cantilever table, which I can readily draw into position or push away, so that I can maintain a strain-free posture whenever I work.

The seat of a normal easy chair is too low, and its back too far away to give support. Such a set-up leads to the knees being cocked in the air, the abdomen being folded, which restricts normal functions such as digestion and breathing, and the spine being curved in an effort to find support: all-in-all a close approximation to the foetal crouch, but without the support of amniotic fluid!

Have you ever used a nice smooth ruler as a straight-edge, and had it slip at the last moment, leaving a line sweeping off the straight at the end? This is how I avoid it.

I take a rigid metal ruler, or any rigid piece of metal that is straight, and use this instead of a plastic or wooden ruler. I buy a sheet of the finest grade of sandpaper or carborundum paper I can find (sometimes called flour grade), and I glue a strip of this to the back of the straight-edge, scoring the non-sanded side and snapping off any surplus. I tidy up any overhang and finally take off the extreme sharpness of the paper by gently rubbing it with a spare piece of itself.

Such a straightedge stays in its place on paper, card, and cloth, enabling you to mark straight lines with pencil, ballpoint, chalk, knife or rotary cutter, without slipping and without the fabric bunching up underneath it. The one I made 20 years ago, although apparently quite smooth, still works.

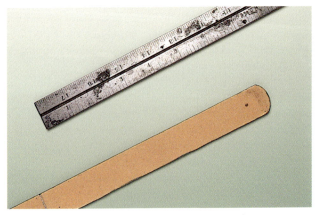

Non-slip straightedge, front and back

Sealing Edges

Sealing fabric edges with adhesive

If an embroidery is to be cut out for use in appliqué, I like to seal its edges to prevent the ground fabric fraying, and to secure the embroidery threads against accidental snipping.

If I intend to mount the item on a backing, for example a brooch or hair comb, I rely on the adhesive to be used in mounting it, usually Evostik Impact Adhesive, to seal its edges. In other cases I use a dilute PVA emulsion, and smear it into the back of the embroidery, only at the edges and only enough to penetrate the ground fabric, but not the actual embroidery. The edge stitches benefit from being fixed in case they get snipped when cutting the motif out, but the main areas of embroidery should not require fixing.

While the PVA will eventually wash out, if the embroidery is well sewn on, no harm should come to it – one of my butterflies has been on the pocket of an oft-washed shirt for two or three years with no harm done.

See also
Adhesives
(page 3)

Shisha Mirrors

Traditionally, the little mirrors known as shisha were pieces of natural mica. A few of these are still commercially available, but it is now more common to find mirror glass as a shisha substitute. Mirror glass has been used in the cushion and jewellery box shown in A.

Modern synthetic packaging provides another alternative. There are a number of heavyweight, shiny plastic films made (as seen in B), which can be cut up and used in place of true shisha mica. They come in various shades of gold and silver, and also in delicate greens and blues.

It is worth keeping an eye open for such unusual, but attractive materials – add them to your stocks of 'I don't know what I can use it for, but I like it' materials.

A Mirror glass used for decoration

B Shiny plastic film can be used in place of shisha

Singeing to Remove Fuzz

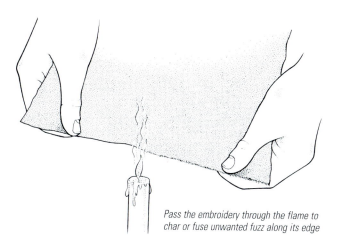

Pass the embroidery through the flame to char or fuse unwanted fuzz along its edge

Sometimes an embroidery that has been cut out has a fuzz of fibres around its edges. A simple way of removing these is to singe them.

If you have a gas cooker, light a ring, and pass the embroidery over the flame. (If you don't have a gas cooker use a candle.) If you are too quick nothing will happen, if you are too slow you will scorch your embroidery, but if you judge it correctly, the loose fibres will char or fuse (depending on whether they are cotton, wool, or synthetic), and no harm will come to the actual stitching.

This principle was used in making the finest grade of cotton sewing threads, called 'gassed threads', where the spun thread was passed at high speed over gas flames, to remove any minute, but unwanted fuzz.

Squaring-Up

Working out your own design may start with getting the image to the scale you want. I have worked on panels 6ft (1.8m) tall, and on miniatures only a few inches across. The scale of your work will depend upon the subject, and your choice of technique.

It is so easy to adapt the scale of an image to suit your needs. The method I use is called 'squaring-up'. It consists of covering the original image with a grid of squares, and copying the detail in each square into another grid of squares, either larger or smaller, according to whether the image is to be scaled up or down.

It is not necessary to deface the original image by marking the grid directly on it. On a piece of paper, draw a grid in the scale you want, and tape a piece of firm, clear plastic over this. The lid of a confectionery box is ideal. With the point of a needle, carefully score over the lines of the grid onto the plastic, rub a little soft pencil lead over this, and with a fingertip, work the lead into the lines and wipe off any excess. You now have a grid which, taped over your original subject, breaks it up into squares.

On another sheet of paper, big enough to take the blown up version of the image if it is to be enlarged, draw a similar grid of larger or smaller squares. If, for example, you wanted to make an embroidery three times the size of the original, you would make the squares in the second grid three times the size of those covering the subject. The number of squares should be the same.

Now, starting with the top left-hand square of the subject, fill in the detail in the top left-hand square of the second grid, in due proportion. You need only fill in the detail required to guide your embroidery. Move on to the next square, and so on, noting the detail you need from the squares of the original subject in the corresponding squares of the copy.

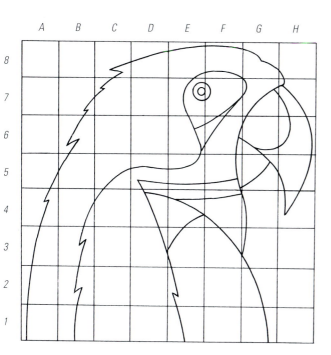

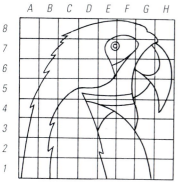

43

Stiletto

I nstead of using an orthodox metal stiletto, I make my own stilettos from a piece of hardwood. I take a piece some 4in (10cm) long, the thickness of a large pencil, and taper it along its length, to a fine point. With this I can make a hole of any size, from a little bigger than that made by a needle, up to one large enough to take a bold cord, depending on how far I insert the stiletto into the cloth.

I rub the stiletto on a bit of beeswax before making the hole and, using a twisting motion, leave a trace of wax around its edges. This stops the divided threads closing in before I make use of the hole.

To prevent the stiletto rolling about, I plane or sand a flat edge along one side.

Tapered wooden stiletto

See also
Knotted Threads
(page 26)

Straightening a Warped Embroidery

There are many embroideries tucked away, with disappointment, because they finished up warped. Typically, uni-directional stitches, on an inadequately supported ground cloth, have caused tensions that have pulled the embroidery out of shape. Many books will tell you to pin such an item out to its desired shape, and then to dampen it, and all will be well. However, this only seems to work if the distortion is slight, in which case it could probably be corrected in the course of mounting. This is the method I use:

1   Measure the work along its sides.

2   Take four pieces of wood at least 2in (50mm) longer than the measurements of the embroidery, and assemble them to form a frame with the inside measurements 1in (25mm) less than the embroidery.

3   Fix the frame sides together with a single nail or screw where they cross.

4   Push the frame to the existing shape of the embroidery, and staple or pin the work to it, with two sides of the embroidery fixed under the top sides of the frame, and the other two sides of the embroidery fixed on top of the bottom sides of the frame. Leave about $\frac{1}{2}$ in (13mm) of the work on the frame all around. Keep the work flat and under some tension.

5   Thoroughly dampen the work, by either spraying or spongeing it.

6   Ease the frame, and the work inside it, back to the desired shape and a bit beyond. This is important, as it is necessary to allow for some give for the eventual relaxation of the frame.

7   Tie a length of string across the short diagonal of the frame to hold it in its new position, and leave the embroidery to dry.

Continued...

8   When quite dry, untie the string. If the embroidery springs back too far, dampen it again, and repeat the process.

9   When a satisfactory shape has been achieved, remove the work from the straightening frame, and mount it on a rectangular frame, board or card.

Measure the length and width of the embroidery

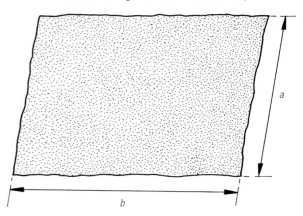

a

b

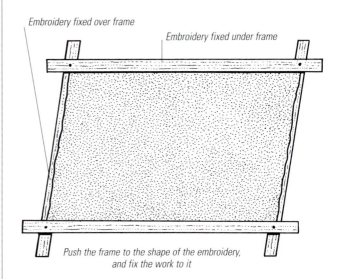

Embroidery fixed over frame

Embroidery fixed under frame

Push the frame to the shape of the embroidery, and fix the work to it

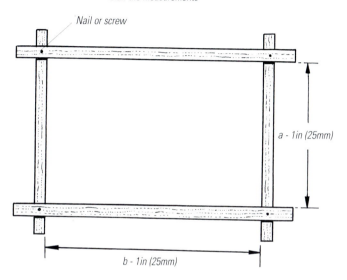

Assemble a frame 1in (25mm) smaller
than the measurements

Nail or screw

a - 1in (25mm)

b - 1in (25mm)

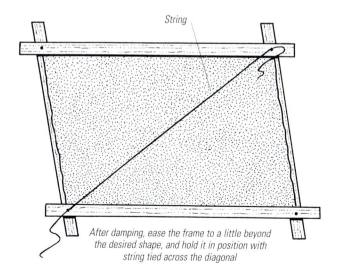

String

After damping, ease the frame to a little beyond
the desired shape, and hold it in position with
string tied across the diagonal

See also
Double Ground
(page 18)
Evening Tension
(page 20)

Supporting the Workpiece

For much of my work I use an up-and-down stab stitch, with one hand above and one hand below the embroidery. This is fast and accurate, and makes full use of both hands instead of using one merely to hold the work.

Using a framed workpiece, I let the frame overhang the edge of a table, with a heavy weight on the back to hold it down. My favourite weight is a piece of scrap iron weighing about 2lb (1kg), which I have wrapped in leather for decency's sake. A heavy book, or something similar can be used instead. My weight also has a bent pin in its cover: this is what I call my third hand. To stop the frame shifting, and to avoid it rattling against the table, I stick bits of squidge to its corners.

Praying mantises and clips holding the workpiece in place

For some pieces, especially larger ones, I use a development of the weighted frame. I do not get on with conventional standing frames – perhaps I am too vigorous, but they always wobble. Instead, I fix together pieces of wood to make 'praying mantises', fix the working frame to two such creations, and fix them to the table, either with heavy weights or with strong spring clips. Such an arrangement enables me to work in my usual stab-stitch way, with no impediment to free access, either above or below the workpiece. It also enables me to maintain a good posture and to have a clear view of the work.

See also
Adapting Equipment
(page 2)
Posture
(page 37)
Third Hand
(page 54)

Tailors' Chalk

Tailors' chalk is supplied coated with a waxy substance to prevent the chalk soiling one's fingers when in use. Before using it, scrape off this coating from both sides of one edge, leaving a sharp, chisel point: this will give a clear, fine line instead of the broad, fuzzy line produced by an unprepared edge.

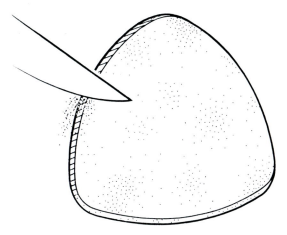

Remove the waxy substance from one edge of the chalk to give a sharp point

I find bulldog clips very useful. One of the ways in which I use them is to provide temporary 'tacking'. Stitching patchwork, I used to find myself with too little turning left at the last edge, when tacking a patch to its pattern. Now I use a bulldog clip to hold the last edge to the pattern while I tack around the rest of it, as shown in A. I also use a bulldog clip to hold down the 'ears' while I sew sharp-cornered patches together as in B, and for holding 'ears' out of the way of the loop of thread while I stitch.

In general, bulldog clips can be used to provide a temporary attachment in any situation where pinning or actual tacking are less convenient.

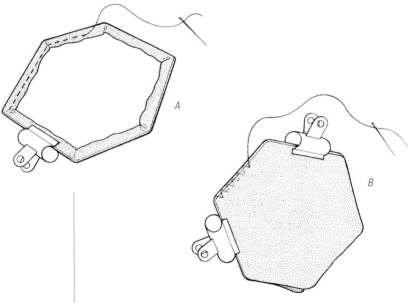

A

B

See also
**Drawing Out a
Single Thread**
(page 19)

Temporary Tensioners

I use Lastex, or shirring elastic, to make temporary tensioners. I take two pins and bend them at the tips to form hooks. I then join these pins with a length of Lastex to form a tensioner, as shown in A.

I use several such tensioners to hold fabrics in place while I work on them, for example: to hold a piece of net, gauze or chiffon over another fabric while I stitch it down as an overlay (shown in B); to hold a top fabric in position over the ground fabric while quilting a cushion cover; and for any situation where I want something held in position, while retaining enough freedom to 'give'.

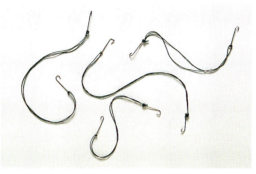

A *Lastex and pin tensioners*

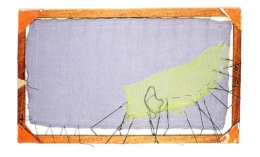

B *Temporary tensioners in use*

Steel dressmakers' pins will snap if you try to bend them, but plated brass or mild steel pins work well. The plating may crack, but the pins shouldn't snap.

See also
Defining a Straight Line
(page 17)
Double Ground
(page 18)

Sometimes, if there is a tendency for it to cockle, I want to ensure that a finished work is kept under tension after it has been finished and backed. In such a case, I turn in and iron the backing, to make it about ¼ in (6mm) smaller than the work in each direction, and stitch through the backing and well into the work, drawing the materials together under tension as I stitch. If the work is on a thick board or frame, I stitch about half-way down the thickness, drawing it up towards the backing.

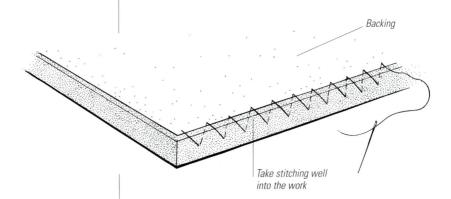

Backing

Take stitching well
into the work

See also
Backing Cloth
(page 6)

Thimbles

Doing a lot of embroidery, I often need to protect my fingers by using a thimble. I have not yet found a thimble to fit, as thimbles are always shaped like cones, and my fingers are not conical. Metal or plastic thimbles not only tend to fall off, they also make my fingers sweat.

My answer is to cut the fingers off an old pair of stout leather gloves, and to secure the glove finger to my finger with a thread of Lastex around the bottom, below a knuckle joint – in effect, making a fingerstall. This is dense enough for all but the heaviest work, where I would probably use pliers to push the needle through anyway.

Having done this for years, I found my local haberdasher offering leather thimbles for about £2 each, crudely made in Korea, specifically for quilters!

Thimble made from leather glove

Third Hand

A The third hand – combined weight and hook

I use a heavy weight to hold a working frame on the table. I have covered this weight in leather, and stuck a bent pin in the end of it. The whole contraption is what I call my third hand, and is shown in A.

I use this third hand in many ways: to secure any piece of fabric which I want to keep taut while I work on it; to help ease one piece of cloth onto another, slightly smaller piece, as shown in B; to hold two pieces of fabric together while I tack or oversew them; to hold a seam taut while I unpick or pull it open; and innumerable other small uses.

To hold a piece of fabric taut while I work, I fix the right-hand side to the hook on the weight, and hold the other side with my left hand, keeping the fabric under tension, and using my right hand to do the pinning or sewing.

Easing one piece of cloth onto another helps when one has to join a piece of fabric cut on the straight of the weave, to one cut on the bias (two gores, triangular or tapered pieces), as there is a tendency for the bias edge to stretch, although cut to the correct length. Tacking the

See also
Frames
(page 21)

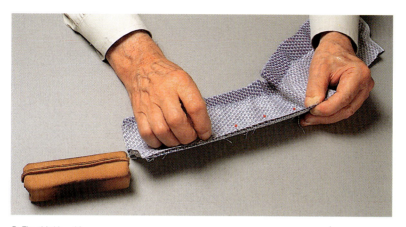

B The third hand in use

stretched piece into the exact position on the smaller piece keeps them in the right relationship as you sew them together.

When not in use, I turn the pin in, and tuck it into the leather for safety.

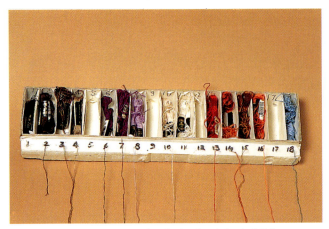

Storing threads in a 'palette'

As I often work with a number of coloured threads, some of them of very similar tones, I find it a great help to use what I call my palette. This is a simple, divided box made of folded paper or thin card, with each division 1 x 1½ x 3in (25 x 38 x 76mm) deep. I have 18 such compartments in a box 18 x 3 x 1½ in (457 x 76 x 38mm). On the front of the box, I have a piece of expanded polystyrene.

In each compartment I keep a skein of stranded cotton, together with the partly-used length of that colour, if there is one. In front of each compartment, I keep a needle for that colour, stuck in the polystyrene.

This palette keeps the threads tidy and separate, yet all available, and the needles tell me which colour I have in use at the time – if there is a needle missing, that is the colour in use. For smaller jobs I have similar palettes, but with only six compartments.

When a job is finished, I wrap the remaining length of cut thread around the folded skein, before returning it to a plastic storage bag, of which I have a number, each for a family of colours, all stored in 2l. (4pt.) ice-cream containers. Using this method of storage, I have no trouble with tangled yarns.

To make such a box, draw out a plan as illustrated, cut along the solid lines, and score and fold along the broken lines. Fold and glue together the two end pairs, and each of the side pairs. Fold up the back and front pieces, then turn in the tabs and fix them to these backs and fronts.

		Tab	Back	Tab	Tab	Back	
End	End			Side 1	Side 1		x
		Tab	Front	Tab	Tab	Front	

Each compartment takes 4in (10cm) of paper and card, so you may need to join pieces together in order to make as many compartments as you require. The easiest way to do this, is to finish each piece at the top of a side (marked 'x' on the plan), and join the next piece to this with the other half of the side.

Tool Boxes

I have made toolboxes to a design worked out between an assiduous daughter-in-law and myself, for various members of the family. Hers is about 24 x 12 x 12in (61 x 31 x 31cm), but I have made smaller boxes.

The general design is a box with its lid split across the centre so that each half can fold back fully. Each lid half is fitted with ridged felt to hold needles and pins. The body of the box carries a tray with a hole in the middle. The tray can accommodate the most used threads and tools, with the central hole enabling the work-in-progress to be stored easily between sessions.

My own toolbox is quite different, as I concentrate on embroidery and do little general sewing. My box is smaller, being only 12 x 6 x 4in (31 x 15 x 10cm). The lid is split in the middle as for the other boxes, but the front half opens to fall down the front of the box, and the back half opens against a stay, to stand almost upright, as can be seen in A. Both halves are fitted with ridged felt to hold needles. In the back lid I keep 'specials', arranged in groups: glovers, leather, curved, and large upholstery needles (18); beading straws (17); and then sharps and betweens grouped by size (36). In the front lid I keep crewels from 8s to 4s, and upwards to long darners (56); and tapestries from 26s to 22s, along with individual larger needles (42). In total, I have 151 needles in my toolbox lid, and more that I keep inside.

A Tool box adapted to suit embroiderers' needs

The main body of the box is composed of three sections, which can be seen in B: a tray, which has a rounded base to prevent small things getting lost in its corners, and which I have mounted on legs to keep it clear of the bottom of the box; a clear plastic box with a hinged lid (I used an old confectionery box); and the general body of the box itself.

I use the tray to hold all the tools I use frequently: 5in (127mm) general purpose scissors; curved nail scissors; bulldog clips; leather thimbles; wooden stiletto; seam ripper; stitch cutter; tweezers (spade end, pointed, and oblique); plastic slip; very fine crochet hook; needle in holder (very fine spike); $3\frac{1}{2}$ in (89mm) pointed embroidery scissors; ball of beeswax; and Fred. Between the tray and the sides of the toolbox are cutting-out scissors, and pinking shears.

In the ex-confectionery box are the tools I use less often: five colours of tailors' chalk; spool of polyester button thread for lashing, with a card of short pieces of the thread, ready for re-use; spool of Lastex shirring elastic; measuring tape; snap-off craft knife; razor blade (securely covered); ring of assorted safety pins; brush for removing chalk marks; wire brush for use as a teasel; pack of putty rubber; piece of cork; three rubber bands; metal sheath thimble; and magnet.

B The three sections of the tool box

In the bottom of the toolbox I keep the tools I seldom use: home-made upholstery needle (which I used for buttoning thick cushions before I acquired a double-pointed upholstery needle, Victorian and beautifully made); 11in (28cm) latched needle, with a ring on the end for pulling tubes inside out; ring of nappy pins with covered heads (I've forgotten what I used these for); box of Lastex tensioners; long hook; chalk pencil with a brush on the end; stiff wire brush; bias binding marker; electric torch (for locating dropped needles); magnifying glass; pricker/marker wheel; and a pack of special tools, comprising four sizes of sack needles, a bodkin, a 5in (127mm) fine needle, a 3in (76mm) tapestry needle, a latched needle, and three hooks.

My toolbox is great fun, and most of these tools are useful, but the fact remains that the only essential tool is a needle!

See also
Defining a Straight Line
(page 17)
Double Ground
(page 18)
Fred: Catching Scraps of Thread
(page 23)
Temporary Tensioners
(page 51)

Transferring Designs

There are several ways of transferring designs to the working fabric, the least satisfactory, from my point of view, being pouncing. This involves pricking through a paper pattern, and rubbing pounce (powder) through the pricked holes: with me, the powder always bounces off before I can translate the design into tacking.

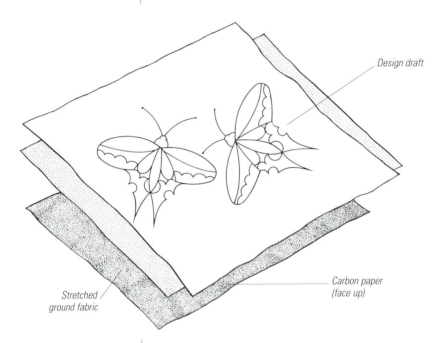

Design draft

Carbon paper
(face up)

Stretched
ground fabric

One method I occasionally use, is to tack through the pattern, and eventually tear away the paper to leave the tacking as the design. The tacking stitches need to be small, otherwise they flop about when the paper has been torn off, as this stretches them a little. The paper should be readily tearable, and it helps if, after tacking, the design is followed by pressing the point of a needle along the outline, under the tacking thread, to score the paper before tearing it.

Usually, I transfer the design using carbon paper (known as tracing paper in the USA). This is available from haberdashers, often in packs of red, blue or orange, and occasionally also in white and yellow. If none of these colours are suitable, I make my own paper by rubbing ordinary wax crayons onto firm wax paper, for example, draughtsman's tracing paper, drafting paper, kitchen paper, or layout paper. In this way, I can choose the colour I use so that, if some of the transferred design is not covered by the embroidery, it will be inconspicuous.

If it is important not to have any of the transferred design showing, I lay the carbon paper face upwards underneath the stretched ground fabric, and place the design draft over that. I then trace through so that the design, in reverse, prints onto the back of the ground fabric. This works well with a thin ground fabric, but with a thick fabric it is difficult to get a good trace. The outline can then be followed with tacking, which will show on the front as your guide, and which can be removed after the embroidery has been done, to avoid any uncovered tacking showing through.

Tweezers

My fingers are somewhat clumsy, and picking up small tools can sometimes be a bit of a fiddle. Moreover, the natural animosity of inanimate things makes them roll out of the way whenever they have a chance!

For frequently used tools such as tweezers, I have an answer. I stick little, flat pieces of wood on either side of them: this stops them rolling, and makes them much easier to pick up and use.

I also do this with fine hooks, as it makes it easier to tell which way the actual hook is facing.

Wood 'casing' makes tools easier to pick up and use

Washing & Dusting Embroideries

All textiles lose some of their strength when wet (up to 60% with some fabrics), and they can hold up to 10 times their weight in water. Obviously this increase in weight, coupled with the loss in strength, necessitates care in washing frail or delicate fabrics, in order to avoid damage or distortion.

A Nylon curtain stretched across a frame to form a screen

The traditional way to wash a Shetland shawl or bedjacket was to fill the sink or bowl with soapy water, and place a tea towel in it, across its base. The shawl was then placed in the suds, gently squeezed until it was clean, and lifted out by the tea towel. Rinsing was done in the same way, so that at no time was the weight of the shawl borne by the fabric. Less delicate items were washed inside a pillowslip.

B For protection, embroideries are washed between screens

Delicate embroidery must be given the same care. When handling old samplers and other delicate fabrics, which have first been checked for colour fastness, I use conservation screens, shown in A. I make these by stretching a piece of nylon curtain net across a simple frame, and pinning, stapling or lashing it in place. I generally make frames about 12 x 6in (30.5 x 15cm). I place the article between two such screens, as in B, and wash and rinse it thus fully supported and under no stress. I finish by dabbing out any excess moisture, and leaving it to dry, still in its sandwich.

Continued…

C Vacuum cleaning through a net screen

Conservation screens can also be used for dusting embroideries. I prefer not to glaze my embroideries, because I like them to be seen without reflections in the glass, and I like the textures to be felt, if the materials can stand it. This means that my works do get dusty, so from time to time I dust them.

I lay a screen on the embroidery and vacuum through it, as shown in C. The net doesn't interfere with the efficiency of the vacuum, but it does avoid surface abrasion, and it prevents any threads being disturbed or drawn up with the suction.

See also
**Colour
Fastness Test**
(page 11)

Index

Harold Hayes spent his working life in an industry dominated by repeated manual operations, where it was his responsibility to ensure that avoidable frustrations were removed. Working in laundering and dry-cleaning, he also worked with every sort of textile. On retiring, he made a loom and began to weave his own fabrics, including tapestries, for subsequent embellishment with embroidery.

Embroidery took over completely, and for the last 15 years has been his main occupation. Harold has talked, demonstrated and exhibited to Embroiderers' Guild branches, schools and other groups throughout the south-east of England, sharing the knowledge he has gained, and the personal methods he has developed over this time.

He exhibits his work whenever and wherever there is an opportunity, and sells enough for what has become his obsession to be self-supporting.

TITLES AVAILABLE FROM GUILD OF MASTER CRAFTSMAN PUBLICATIONS

BOOKS

The Art of the Woodcarver
GMC Publications
Carving Birds and Beasts
GMC Publications
Faceplate Turning: Features, Projects, Practice
GMC Publications
Practical Tips for Turners & Carvers
GMC Publications
Useful Woodturning Projects
GMC Publications
Woodturning Techniques
GMC Publications
Woodworkers' Career and Educational Source Book
GMC Publications
Woodworkers' Courses & Source Book
GMC Publications
Woodworking Crafts Annual
GMC Publications
Woodworking Plans and Projects
GMC Publications
40 More Woodworking Plans and Projects
GMC Publications
Green Woodwork Mike Abbott
Easy to Make Dolls' House Accessories Andrea Barham
Making Little Boxes from Wood John Bennett
Woodturning Masterclass Tony Boase
Furniture Restoration and Repair for Beginners
Kevin Jan Bonner
Woodturning Jewellery Hilary Bowen
The Incredible Router Jeremy Broun
Electric Woodwork Jeremy Broun
Woodcarving: A Complete Course Ron Butterfield
Making Fine Furniture: Projects Tom Darby
Restoring Rocking Horses Clive Green & Anthony Dew
Heraldic Miniature Knights Peter Greenhill
Make Your Own Dolls' House Furniture Maurice Harper
Practical Crafts: Seat Weaving Ricky Holdstock
Multi-centre Woodturning Ray Hopper
Complete Woodfinishing Ian Hosker

Practical Crafts: Woodfinishing Handbook Ian Hosker
Woodturning: A Source Book of Shapes John Hunnex
Illustrated Woodturning Techniques John Hunnex
Making Shaker Furniture Barry Jackson
Upholstery: A Complete Course David James
Upholstery Techniques and Projects David James
The Uplolsterer's Pocket Reference Book David James
Designing and Making Wooden Toys Terry Kelly
Making Dolls' House Furniture Patricia King
Making Victorian Dolls' House Furniture Patricia King
Making and Modifying Woodworking Tools
Jim Kingshott
The Workshop Jim Kingshott
Sharpening: The Complete Guide Jim Kingshott
Sharpening Pocket Reference Book Jim Kingshott
Turning Wooden Toys Terry Lawrence
Making Board, Peg and Dice Games Jeff & Jennie Loader
Making Wooden Toys and Games Jeff & Jennie Loader
Bert Marsh: Woodturner Bert Marsh
The Complete Dolls' House Book Jean Nisbett
The Secrets of the Dolls' House Makers Jean Nisbett
Wildfowl Carving, Volume 1 Jim Pearce
Wildfowl Carving, Volume 2 Jim Pearce
Make Money from Woodturning Ann & Bob Phillips
Guide to Marketing Jack Pigden
Woodcarving Tools, Materials and Equipment Chris Pye
Carving on Turning Chris Pye
Making Tudor Dolls' Houses Derek Rowbottom
Making Georgian Dolls' Houses Derek Rowbottom
Making Period Dolls' House Furniture
Derek & Sheila Rowbottom
Woodturning: A Foundation Course Keith Rowley
Turning Miniatures in Wood John Sainsbury
Pleasure and Profit from Woodturning Reg Sherwin
Making Unusual Miniatures Graham Spalding
Woodturning Wizardry David Springett
Adventures in Woodturning David Springett
Furniture Projects Rod Wales
Decorative Woodcarving Jeremy Williams

VIDEOS

Dennis White Teaches Woodturning
Part 1 Turning Between Centres
Part 2 Turning Bowls
Part 3 Boxes, Goblets and Screw Threads
Part 4 Novelties and Projects
Part 5 Classic Profiles
Part 6 Twists and Advanced Turning
John Jordan **Bowl Turning**

John Jordan **Hollow Turning**
Jim Kingshott **Sharpening the Professional Way**
Jim Kingshott **Sharpening Turning and Carving Tools**
Ray Gonzalez **Carving a Figure: The Female Form**
David James **The Traditional Upholstery Workshop**
Part I: Drop-in and Pinstuffed Seats
David James **The Traditional Upholstery Workshop**
Part II: Stuffover Upholstery

Guild of Master Craftsman Publications regularly produces new books on a wide range of woodworking and craft subjects, and an increasing number of specialist magazines, all available on subscription:

MAGAZINES

WOODTURNING   WOODCARVING   BUSINESSMATTERS

All these publications are available through bookshops and newsagents,
or may be ordered by post from the publishers at
166 High Street, Lewes, East Sussex BN7 1XU, Telephone (01273) 477374, Fax (01273) 478606
Credit card orders are accepted.

PLEASE WRITE OR PHONE FOR A FREE CATALOGUE